JOURNAL

PETER PAUPER PRESS, INC.
WHITE PLAINS, NEW YORK

Cover image: Gilt morocco binding by Roger Bartlett, Oxford,
on *The Holy Bible* (London, 1678)
The Pierpont Morgan Library, New York. PML 59412/Art Resource, NY

Martck 21st

Reatas

2

21 31
30 30

Msn. thorp

Sticky Ribs

Sauc Susan
dijon mustard
Louisiana Sauce

grape jam

honey
garlic powder

Organic No-Salt Seasoning

Cinnamon

balsamic vinegar

add small bit of
cooking beer

boil ribs in
beer w/pepper
corns + bay
leaves

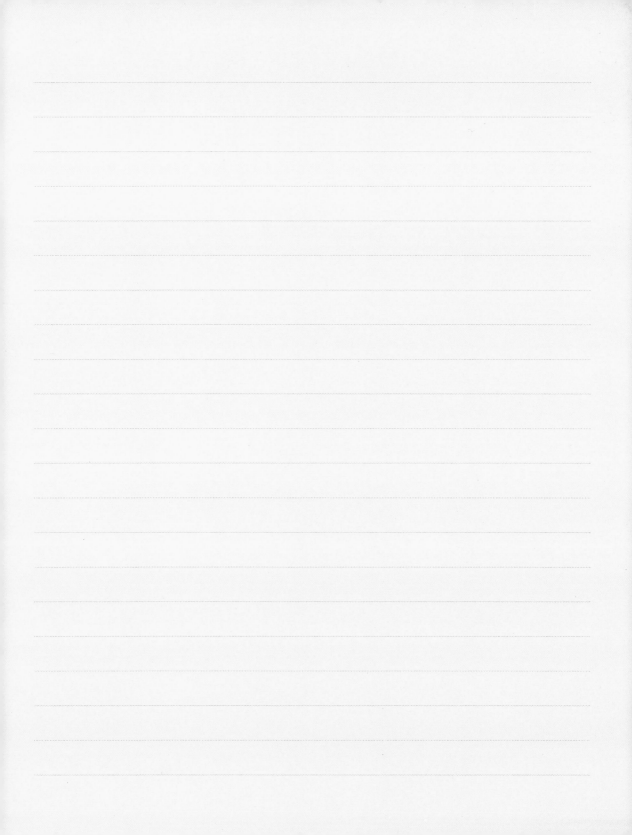

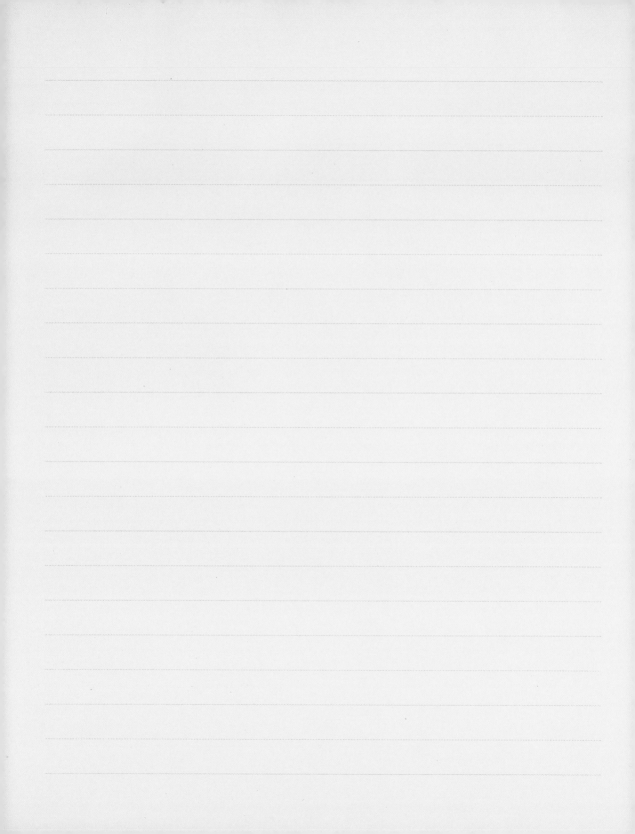